Carolina Friends School
Durham Early School

# my five senses

## by aliki

A Harper Trophy Book

## LET'S-READ-AND-FIND-OUT BOOKS

The *Let's-Read-and-Find-Out* series was founded by Dr. Roma Gans, Professor Emeritus of Childhood Education, Teachers College, Columbia University, and Dr. Franklyn M. Branley, Astronomer Emeritus and former Chairman of the American Museum-Hayden Planetarium. Text and illustrations for each of the more than 100 books in the series are checked for accuracy by an expert in the relevant field. Other titles available in paperback are listed below. Look for them at your local bookstore or library.

My Five Senses
Copyright © 1962 by Aliki
Printed in the U.S.A. All rights reserved.

Library of Congress Catalog Card Number: 62-7150
Trade ISBN 0–690–56762–6
Library ISBN 0–690–56763–4
Trophy ISBN 0–06–445009–0
First Harper Trophy edition, 1985.

my
five
senses

I can see! I see with my eyes.

I can hear! I hear with my ears.

3

I can smell! I smell with my nose.

4

5

I can taste! I taste with my tongue.

8

I can touch! I touch with my fingers.

I do all this with my senses.
I have five senses.

When I see the sun or a bird

or my baby sister,
I use my sense of sight. I am seeing.

11

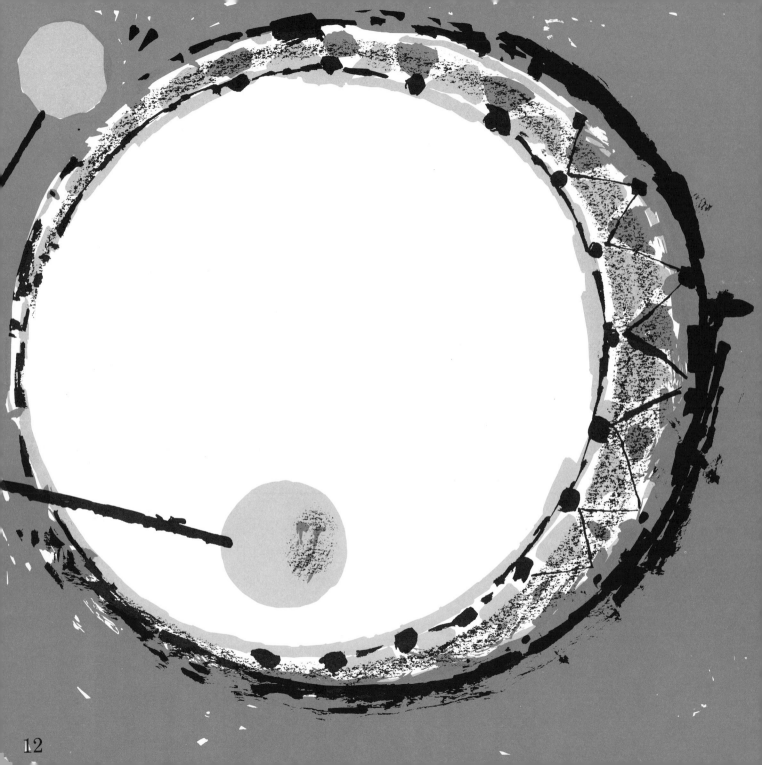

When I hear a drum or a fire engine or an egg beater,
I use my sense of sound. I am hearing.

When I smell baby powder
or a pine tree

or cookies just out of the oven,
I use my sense of smell.
I am smelling.

When I drink my milk and eat my food,
I use my sense of taste. I am tasting.

17

When I touch a kitten

or a balloon or raindrops,
I use my sense of touch.
I am touching.

Sometimes I use all my senses at once.

Sometimes I use only one.

I often play a game with myself.

I guess how many senses I am using, at that time.


When I look at the moon and the stars,

I use one sense.

I am seeing.

When I laugh and play with my puppy,
I use four senses.
I see, hear, smell, and touch.

When I bounce a ball, I use three senses.
I see, hear, touch.

Sometimes I use more of one sense
and less of another.
But each sense is very important to me,
because it makes me aware.

To be aware is to see all there is to see . . .

. . . hear all there is to hear . . .

28

. . . smell all there is to smell . . .

... taste all there is to taste ...

. . . touch all there is to touch.

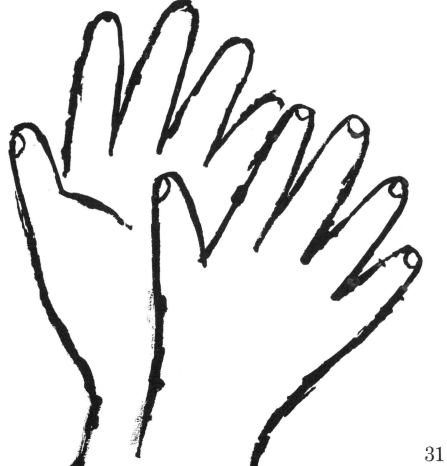

# I SEE  I HEAR  I TASTE  I SMELL  I TOUCH

Wherever I go, whatever I do,
every minute of the day,
my senses are working.

They make me aware.

## ABOUT THE AUTHOR-ILLUSTRATOR

ALIKI uses her five senses the same way she illustrates children's books and pursues commercial art—one or more at a time. She loves music, books, and watching her plants grow.

Aliki Brandenberg grew up in Philadelphia, where she attended the Museum College of Art.

Her extensive European travels include a motor and painting tour from Switzerland, where she lived and worked as an artist for four years, through Italy, Yugoslavia, and Greece.

Mr. and Mrs. Brandenberg now reside in New York City.

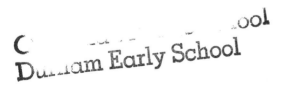